How to
Live Through
a Bad Day

How to
Live Through
a Bad Day

7 Encouraging Insights from
Christ's Words on the Cross

JACK W. HAYFORD

OLIVER
NELSON™

THOMAS NELSON PUBLISHERS
Nashville

Published in Nashville, Tennessee, by Thomas Nelson, Inc.

Scripture quotations are from the NEW KING JAMES VERSION of the Bible. Copyright © 1979, 1980, 1982, Thomas Nelson, Inc., Publishers.

ISBN 0-7852-6617-8
Library of Congress Control Number: 2001 135304

Printed in the United States of America

01 02 03 04 05 QWK 7 6 5 4 3 2

Contents

All personal stories related are true. Except for self references by the writer, names have been changed to protect confidentiality.

Preface

There are reasons Good Friday is called "good," but they are not related to our usual human notions of nice, happy, or comfortable. Rather, the "good" in that day is that it is the day God's love gift of His Son, who arrived in Bethlehem years before, surrendered to death on a Cross in Jerusalem. The "good" is in the Good Shepherd, laying His life down for His sheep. The "good" is in the fact that, at the price of Jesus' lifeblood, forgiveness for my sin and yours is now an abiding provision with eternal hope and promise. Yes, there are reasons to call that Friday "good."

But it was a very bad day.

It was a day bearing the fruit of betrayal. It was a day of lying tongues and compromised courts.

It was a day of brutal beating, of vicious bloodletting. It was a day of screamed curses and angered tyrants. It was a day of mindless mobs and jeering throngs.

It was a day of violence on the heels of rejection. It was a day of stark loneliness in the wake of fleeing friends.

It was a day of dismal darkness, thunder, and earthquake. It was a day of human arrogance and folly—a God-forsaken day in which God Himself was killed as He submitted Himself to the hands of His creatures.

It was a day beyond all others, but it was also a day like a thousand of our own in certain ways.

Bad days are commonplace in our world.

That isn't a cynical observation. It's an honest one. And in many regards, the similarities to the order of things that Jesus endured are very much like those that we often experience when we are going through a bad day. Although the *dimension* of His Good Friday suffering transcends our understanding—just as it has transformed our lives—the *dynamics* of the human experience are often painfully approximate. The epistle to the Philippians refers to it as "the fellowship of His sufferings" (3:10), and that is exactly what Jesus summoned us to discover in answering His call, "Take up your Cross and follow Me." (Matt. 16:24)

His call isn't an idealistic notion; it's a practical pathway. It is our Savior's call to discipleship—the call to "take My yoke upon you and learn from Me . . . and you will find rest for your souls" (Matt. 11:29). In the most final terms, discipleship is the call to Calvary, first and most necessarily to receive the forgiveness and salvation afforded there alone by God's great love. But we are never to remain solely as forgiven penitents. We are called to grow as the Father's sons and daughters, to serve as the King's faithful stewards, to learn as the Master's devoted disciples. And all of that growth, service, and learning is most practically processed not by the way we handle life's blessings, but by the way we live through its bad days.

Bad days happen to everyone. They come more often than we think we deserve, and they sometimes last much longer than we think we can stand. That's the reason every disciple of Jesus needs to have a framework for processing bad days. And God's Word directs us to one: "Let us run with endurance the race that is set before us, looking unto Jesus, the author and finisher of our faith, who for the joy that was set before Him endured the cross" (Heb. 12:1–2).

Are you experiencing one of life's bad days? Then let me invite you to come with me to the Cross, not to commiserate over agonies but to find companionship and direction. While the sum of human pain and problems is focused here—*all* suffering, *all* rejection, *all* painfulness, *all* exhaustion, *all* misunderstanding, *all* anger, *all* hatred, *all* sinning, *all* depression, *all* loneliness, all death—so is *all* wisdom and understanding, with *all* faith, hope, and love. And it is to and by that love most of all that we are summoned to look unto Jesus and to expressly study the way He processed Good Friday—the ultimate bad day. "For the joy that was set before Him [He] endured the Cross," and that explains to us both the *where* and the *why* we are to look. The *where* brings us to His Cross to listen to His words spoken that day, and the *why* is to find hope, for we are specifically told that His endurance that bad day was nourished by a *joy* waiting beyond it.

His promise to each of us is no less—no less than that spoken to a band of exiles being led by their captors from the ruins of their ransacked city, Jerusalem. And it was to the stumbling, shamed platoons of defeated citizens en route to Babylon, seemingly bound by futility and destined to pointlessness, that Jeremiah raised his voice in God's name, declaring,

> I know the thoughts that I think toward you, says the LORD, thoughts of peace and not of evil, to give you a future and a hope. Then you will call upon Me and go and pray to Me, and I will listen to you. And you will seek Me and find Me, when you search for Me with all your heart. I will be found by you, says the LORD, and I will bring you back from your captivity. (Jer. 29:11–14)

The record of history is that God made good that promise, exactly as He assured those people He would on that bad day. And that record isn't there to merely *memorize* as a historic fact; it's given to us to *contemporize*—to apply to our present moment as a prophetic promise! We are called to hope just as surely as we are called to the Cross, for the Savior who speaks there is teaching us the way to live as surely as He is dying to give us life.

Come.

Let us listen and learn, that we may find Love's way to life and living.

Even when life presents us with any dimension of a very bad day.

We will "look unto Jesus" through the lens of that succession of statements He made from the Cross—statements usually referred to as "the seven last words of Christ." The phrase is perfectly understandable, but it is an ill-conceived one, for these are not His final words, nor do they focus finality.

- He will rise in three days: there is much more that He will say—and He is still speaking.

- His "Cross" words are also focused on the future—each statement laden with hope.

We are looking to the *hope unto joy* that brought Him through that day.

Let us begin.

1

Forgive Everyone Who's Trying to Ruin Your Life

Father, forgive them, for they do not know what they do.

—Luke 23:34

Amarvel and a majesty are evident in these first words. The blood of the Lamb had just begun to be spilled from the altar of the Cross. The plan for this moment's provision had moved from Eden's first sacrifice for sin and through centuries of multitudinous animal sacrifices as worshipers were being taught of a Final Sacrifice to come.

He was on the Cross—the Lamb of God who took away the sin of the world.

And He was presenting Himself—the Great High Priest offering His life for mankind's greatest need: forgiveness for sin and release from its bondage.

The first words of this Lamb-Priest are *tender* in the face of His hate-filled antagonists, and they are *timeless* and love-filled as they reach to you and me today. But they are also *teaching* words for us who would be taught how to live through a bad day, and our first lesson is this: To live through a bad day, begin by forgiving everyone who seems to be trying to ruin your life.

It is as common an emotion or as real a reality as any of us experience. Bad days are the results of things that happen, and things that happen are the results of what people do. People who misunderstood. People who intended to hurt us. People who forgot or neglected to do something. People who betrayed or violated us. People whose injury done to us was either yesterday or yesteryear. People do things, and we find it difficult to believe what Jesus said about them that day—that they didn't know what they were doing.

Yet His words are probably the most descriptive truth about all human sin, lovelessness, rebellion, hurt, hate, anger, violence, and the thousand other evils that overflow our fallen race. Even when sin is calculated, planned thoroughly, conceived carefully, and executed efficiently, no one really understands the depth or dimension of sin's destructiveness or the degree of its horrible damage to people. In a very real sense, every sin is a sin of ignorance.

To learn the grace of forgiveness—to embrace the will to forgive anyone or everyone who seems to be ruining your life right now—you need to find a starting place, and Jesus points you to it: "They don't know what they're doing." But the fact of the matter is, that isn't the way you feel. You tend to see things from the viewpoint of your experience, and when bad things happen, it appears that whoever did you wrong knew exactly what he was doing and didn't really seem to care either.

It must have looked that way from the Cross, too, but Jesus teaches about the secret of forgiveness: Forgiving those who assail you is the key to not being permanently victimized by them. Whatever the initial impact of any offense you experience by others, your will to refuse to react, carry a grudge, or seek to retaliate in kind secures the high ground. But it must be as real as the Savior's forgiveness, not merely a humanistically willed exercise in self-control. The latter may appear noble, but it will breed only an internalized pride.

True forgiveness springs from gratitude to God for His forgiving me. True forgiveness is born of my remembrance that I have been forgiven so great a debt through God's love, there is no justification for my being less than fully forgiving to others. Because I have "freely received," my Lord calls me to "freely give." To forgive those seeking to injure you or me is to remove ourselves from their control and to be unfettered by the anger, pain, or disappointment that would seek to attach itself to us.

As I think of the holy reversal brought by a genuine spirit of forgiveness, Richard comes to mind as a marvelous example of such grace. He disallowed the bad day of rejection by a whole circle of friends—one especially—to dominate his heart, and as a result, Richard realized a "new day" for himself and a "happy day" of salvation for another. I heard his story firsthand when he visited my office one day.

It had been nearly two years since Richard had come to Christ. His transformation by the power of the gospel and his rediscovery of the Creator's true design for him as a person—as a man—had produced a true disciple of Jesus. The pathway out of his former lifestyle of living in the West Hollywood community with his male lover had been more than an experimental excursion. As a professional in the medical community, he was respected for his skills. As a member of the homosexual community, he was accepted by a broad circle of like-minded friends. He was the consummate example of all that any community would want to designate as a case study for its effectiveness: "He's a success, and he's one of us!"

The situation changed rapidly, almost viciously, when Richard received Jesus as his Savior. The rejection he experienced had nothing to do with reasons a critic might presume. He became neither a self-righteous judge of his friends nor a preachy saint. But he explained himself to his lover and made every effort to assuage wounded emotions when he announced that he would be discontinuing their relationship. "I care about you, Charles," he said. "But honesty with the truth and faithfulness to the love of God for both of us will not allow me to live as I have anymore. I don't want you to feel I hate you or think you are an unworthy person. I simply know God has a better way for both of us."

The reaction was explosive.

Charles was infuriated and immediately spread the word that Richard had more than simply "done him bad"; he had become one of "them." In the view of hosts of gays, "them" represents those in the Christian community who appear to devalue the humanity of anyone embracing homosexuality. Many do not resent Christians' faith as much as they resent what they regard in many Christians as a loathing, demeaning judgment of them as people. They perceive the epithet *abomination* as a hate-filled, sneering, condescending announcement laced with a social intolerance of individual human rights—motivated by a quest for political control that would exterminate them if Christians ever gained governing power.

And Richard had become one of "them."

Richard's regret was not rooted in the speed with which his many friends turned their backs on him or in the bitterness that virtually spit at his new life of commitment to Christ. Rather he was brokenhearted over the twisted perception of his former friends of what knowing Jesus is really about, and he was equally regretful for the few cases of supposed "Christian" activity that justified the caricature they drew of "them." And that had brought about our meeting in my office that day.

Richard had written me a letter of warm encouragement. He described his having found our church after his conversion to the Savior, and he expressed his deep gratitude for the haven of hope and the atmosphere for growth. He wrote,

> Pastor Jack, it hasn't been easy to find a fellowship that offers both grace and truth. I wanted to

say how thankful I am for a congregation that is constant in both: (1) a commitment to God's Word and its requirements for living in God's will (including the call away from sexual disobedience); and (2) a commitment to God's love and its requirements for showing God's grace to the lost (including a generosity of spirit to all who live in a blindness to their sin—seeking to "love them to life" rather than viewing them with condescension).

I was more heart-warmed by his discerning, solidly discipled understanding than I was by his nice remarks about our church. He was a marvelous case of the way that *Jesus saves*. Those two words that summarize the gospel were in full evidence in this man who had been completely transformed, resurrected from a deadly environment, walking steadfastly in the light of God's Word—a man who was compassionately concerned about those he might reach for Christ, especially those in the grip of his former confusion. Those reasons were heartwarming enough, but I was about to discover something even more profoundly heart stirring.

Our conversation was concluding when Richard made a request. "Before I go, Pastor Jack, would you mind praying with me about something that's happening right now?" I nodded my head, inviting him to go on. "I want to ask your prayer support for the next few days. Let me explain."

He outlined briefly how, only a few weeks before, he had received word that his former lover was dying—now under the siege of a virulent assault of AIDS. Hearing that Charles had virtually disappeared, he went to the apartment they had formerly occupied together and found him there. "I knocked on the door, not only wondering if he was there at all, but feeling very uncertain of what kind of reception I would find if he was," Richard continued.

"When the door cracked open, I was stunned. His face was shriveled; he had open sores; he looked like walking death. As he peered at me through squinting eyes, his face turned to a scowl. He seemed uncertain about opening the door and weakly said, 'Oh, it's you.'"

Richard went on, explaining how Charles had then turned away from the door, but had left it open. "If I hadn't the medical training I do, it would have been dangerous to go in, but I did."

The apartment was in disarray and the stuffiness of the room unpleasant with the smell of death encroaching upon a human body. Richard said nothing, but went about cleaning the place as Charles returned to his bed. With the caution and skill of a professional, Richard proceeded to attend to Charles's needs—helping him bathe, cleansing the sores, remaking his bed, and then preparing a meal for him.

"There were few words exchanged. He was so desperately in need, he could hardly protest the help I was offering, and when I finished washing the dishes, I told him I would be back the next day. Pastor Jack, that was nearly four weeks ago, but my request for prayer is because of what happened this week."

I was already near tears as I listened. The manifest purity of Richard's motives, the gracious compassion in his actions, the clear-eyed concern in his words to me—all were the essence of a Christlike forgivingness.

Here he was, reaching where he had been rejected, loving in the most practical of terms and with the purest of objectives.

"In all these weeks of ministering help to Charles, Pastor, I intentionally did not mention Jesus even once—not because I am ashamed of Him, but because I knew it wouldn't be received. And then, just three days ago, as I was helping Charles back to bed after changing the sheets, he said, almost with pitiful resignation, 'Okay, Richard. Tell me about Jesus.'"

Both Richard's and my eyes were misted as he described Charles's opening his heart to the Savior. And I was overcome with this evidence of the power of forgiveness when it is shown toward the very person who has rejected you.

The request was direct: that we pray for Charles's last days on this earth. Neither Richard nor I was devoid of the belief that Christ can heal, at times even in the most extreme circumstances. And neither of us doubted the possibility of willingness within the mercy of God for one whose condition was the result of so clear a violation of His benevolent intent for mankind.

But there was a sense of closure—one that Charles had expressed, and one to which Richard bore witness—that the physically tormented body about to be left behind was no longer the definition of Charles's future. He had received the Savior. He was ready to go. So, we prayed. Two weeks later, another redeemed soul entered eternal glory, and Richard phoned me to report Charles's homegoing.

The most remarkable thing about that story is the evidence it holds of the sheer power inherent in a disciple's learning the Master's overwhelming, unlimited grace of forgiveness. It is not in denying the bad days that come to us when others reject us or turn on us. It is not in minimizing the pain we experience at the hands of those who seem bent on ruining our lives. People turn on people. Crass unkindness, vicious plottings, horrible and intentional antagonisms are shown, and a bad day hardly describes the extended season of struggle many of us face at times. But there is a lesson at Calvary.

Forgive everyone—anyone—whom you think has failed you, hurt you, offended you. If you think he has done anything to ruin your life, ruin your day, ruin your opportunities, ruin your dreams, or block your goals, forgive him. Forgiving others is the key to living in the liberty of the freeing forgiveness Jesus has given us, and it's the first step toward living through a bad day, not to mention opening the door to new days unimagined.

2

Help Others Who Are Experiencing Your Same Struggle

Assuredly, I say to you, today you will be with Me in Paradise.

—LUKE 23:43

Exactly how soon the interchange took place isn't clear, but Jesus—suspended on a Cross between a pair of thieves also being crucified—was made the subject of a brief debate between the two. Luke's report reads:

Then one of the criminals who were hanged blasphemed Him, saying, "If You are the Christ, save Yourself and us." But the other, answering, rebuked him, saying, "Do you not even fear God, seeing you are under the same condemnation? And we indeed justly, for we receive the due reward of our deeds; but this Man has done nothing wrong." Then he said to Jesus, "Lord, remember me when You come into Your kingdom." And Jesus said to him, "Assuredly, I say to you, today you will be with Me in Paradise." (Luke 23:39–43)

At the beginning of the interchange, Jesus was only an observer-listener. He was on the Cross, but there were two others on crosses to the right and the left. They were criminals, and in an apparent coincidence of scheduling within the Roman program of execution, Jesus' bad day happened to be their day of destruction as well. Both men seemed to be aware of the claims that were made about Jesus and knew why He was there. But only one displayed cynicism and anger, swearing at Jesus and making a mocking reference to His power. The other criminal briskly challenged his counterpart: "Don't you have any respect? This Man doesn't deserve that kind of cynicism or bitterness. He hasn't done anything, but we're getting what we deserve." It was a clear confession of his sinfulness. Then in the same repentant spirit, and with a distinct and humble acknowledgment of Jesus' divinity, he made a request of the Savior: "Lord, remember me when You come into Your kingdom."

Jesus' response is a study in divine mercy, in grace's readiness to give salvation, in God's immeasurable gentleness toward all who come to Him, and in the truth that it is never too late to seek God. It is a scenario that jangles the nerves of the religionist who would haltingly dispense salvation. It is as dramatic a statement that God's Son could make to say, "Those who come to Me, I'll never turn away." That's the gospel truth wrapped in this event, but there's a discipling principle as well. In Jesus' response to this bad day encounter, we're taught a second lesson in how to live through such days of our own: Encourage others who are struggling or uncertain.

Note two elements of Jesus' interaction with the repentant thief. First, the man was experiencing exactly the same thing Jesus was. Please capture that. Jesus could have been focused on His own problems, but He demonstrated sensitivity that remained available to the needs of other people around Him, even while dealing with His own pain. And in that action there was something more.

Second, Jesus might have regarded Himself as the man's superior, but He readily responded as One engaged in the same bad day struggle. True, the thief was facing the day with infinitely fewer resources than Jesus had. Jesus was suffering, but He was—and is—the Lord; even the thief recognized that. Jesus had been pierced at hands and feet with nails, and tortured with a thorn crown crushed onto His head, but He is God's King. Yet it was not from either His spiritually royal role or as a moral superior that the Savior related to the one seeking succor for his soul. He met the man on the common plane of their suffering together on that bad day. Jesus charted the way for our learning that, whatever our bad day may involve, He's calling us to meet fellow strugglers where they are, refusing to distance ourselves by reason of any position or resources we may have. Within God's grace

I've slowly learned this lesson. And on one occasion I was literally shaken up as God exposed me to horrifying fear to help me learn it.

Ten thousand freight trains seemed to be thundering through our home at the moment Los Angeles was so violently devastated. It was 4:31, Monday morning, January 17, 1994, when the Northridge earthquake exploded life at a dimension resulting in one of the most cataclysmically expensive natural disasters in American history. My personal experience is unforgettable in a number of ways, but none more awkward than in the emotional trauma I found myself carrying in the days that immediately followed.

It was embarrassing.

Here I was, a man of faith, solidly established in the spiritual resources of God's Word and charged with the leadership of a flock in need of my strength and ministry to encourage them during the aftermath of the disaster—yet I was terrified. Every jolting aftershock jarred the raw sensitivities of us all, but I doubt that anyone was more traumatized than I was.

I had not been injured, and I had not suffered a

staggering loss as those whose businesses had been left in shambles or those who had been hurt in the quake. Nor was I among the scores left bereaved by the loss of loved ones killed in incidents related to the massive upheaval. Our family was safe, our home virtually untouched beyond some ruined furniture, scattered like toys across the rooms of our home. Still, as night fell on each following day, I seemed to become another person.

Nevertheless, I didn't want to admit to myself, much less to my wife or others, how the inner turmoil seemed to dominate me. It was not quite paralyzing, but it radically inhibited my normal feelings and responses. A trip alone to the other end of the house, especially after dark, nearly terrorized me. Though accustomed to rising in the night to spend an hour or more at prayer in the darkness while the rest of my family slept, I would venture only to the bathroom in the night with a flashlight in hand, and even then I was gripped by a sense of fear I had never known.

After four days of those uncharacteristic feelings, I desperately sought God in prayer. I was not frantic, and I was not stampeded by panic, but I was very,

very bewildered. "Lord," I exclaimed, "I can't understand myself! I am *not* afraid for my life, and I am
not in doubt of Your presence and protection. Please
help me, Lord. I need Your help. Is something wrong
with me?"

Instantly, and with utmost surprise at the imme-
diacy of the response, I sensed an inner whisper to my
soul: *My son, there is nothing wrong with you. I allowed
you to experience the depth of the trauma and fear that
has gripped multitudes so that you might understand
their torment and comfort them beyond their fears.*

I knew that Voice, and I was immediately drawn
to His Word: "Blessed be the God and Father of our
Lord Jesus Christ, the Father of mercies and God of
all comfort, who comforts us in all our tribulation,
that we may be able to comfort those who are in any
trouble, with the comfort with which we ourselves
are comforted by God" (2 Cor. 1:3–4). It relates one
of the classic strategies of the Most High, who uses
His children who have endured difficulty to become
strength to others experiencing the same trial. It is
the divine reminder that we comfort others not from

the foundation of our superior faith but from the commonality of our mutual struggles.

The following week I brought one of the most successful sermons of my forty years of pastoral preaching, "Discerning and Dealing with Fears," teaching from 1 John 4:17–19. Not only did I root my teaching in God's unshakable Word of promise, but I illustrated it with full, personal transparency—relating my own wrestlings with fear over the preceding days. I risked seeming less than a pillar of strength, opened my heart to vulnerably admitting my bewilderment with my apparently less-than-faith-filled nights of uneasiness and the completely unnerving sense of helplessness I felt with every aftershock, and people were strengthened! Hearts took hope. Eyes began to shine again. Faith was evoked in the wake of my confessing my fears. It seemed paradoxical, but it was the fulfillment of God's Word—the one source where faith can be found when bad days surround you.

The elders of our church agreed to provide for thousands of audiocassette copies of my message to be duplicated and distributed freely via our congregation.

Hundreds used them to answer their own inner struggles, while hundreds more passed them on to friends and relatives who were experiencing postquake trauma. The impact was dramatic. And the reason was basically that one lone disciple, tormented by fear where others might have thought him above such distress, was given grace to live out a little of the greatness seen in our great Savior.

That grace is seen most grandly in the midst of the initial Good Friday—the one bad day beyond all bad days. As the Son of God assured another fellow sufferer in the middle of His own agony, He not only comforted him with the promise of eternal hope; He met him in the "today" of his struggle with divine promise, the ultimate assurance: "Assuredly . . . today!" Those are words to take anyone through any bad day.

3

Be Sure You've Taken Care of Those Near You

Woman, behold your son! . . . Behold your mother!

—JOHN 19:26–27

The third key for how to live through a bad day is to be sure you've taken care of those near you. Its wisdom flows from the motive and moment of these gentle directives. From the Cross, Jesus first addressed Mary, His mother. Then He spoke to John, the only one of His twelve disciples who followed Jesus all the way to the Cross.

For various reasons Jesus' others disciples fled—mostly out of fear. But John stayed with Him—first following Him to the place of His trial and then to the scene of His crucifixion. There were also three women at the Cross, probably having joined John earlier in the day at his request. Most notably, considering the pathos of the moment, one of them was Jesus' mother, and the two other women were probably there to attend to her. To watch your child tortured unto death was heavy fare for anyone, and supportive friends were needed.

Mary is an interesting study throughout the life of Jesus. She became a disciple of her own son. Mary was never confused about her role in relation to Jesus. From the beginning she knew the difference between who *she* was and who *He* was. And when we read of her presence at His death—a brave and noble act, to say the least—we would be blinded by bigotry or devoid of human sensitivity not to sympathize with the mother's heartache as she watches her son bear the agony and the torment of His Cross.

That is all very meaningful and quite emotional

when we think about it from Mary's side—feeling with her as her maternal instincts were being ripped to shreds. But another matter is present here, probably not dominant in her mind, but inevitably an issue to be faced sooner than later: "When He's gone, what is going to happen to me?"

Because Jesus was her oldest child, Mary was essentially subordinate to and dependent upon His care, most likely for years. Most scholars suggest that Joseph was much older than Mary, and that following his death, Jesus had taken up leadership of his business as well as responsibility for leading the family. So now, on the brink of death, is the One who would have been her protector, her "covering" as we often say, especially in a society where women were so frequently disenfranchised by the deaths of the men in their lives. Thus, however noble her maternal concern, there cannot help but have been an uncertainty in Mary's future. And again, this Man—God in our midst, Jesus—teaches us more about living through a bad day.

Though surrounded by turmoil and the swirling

of events targeting His destruction, Jesus turned His concern to His mother's personal plight. When He said, "Woman, behold your son!" He wasn't saying, "Look at Me and weep, Mother." He was directing her attention to John. He was saying, "Woman [a term of respect, approximately equivalent to ma'am], this man will become the one to oversee you." And completing the transfer of responsibility for His mother, He said to John, "Son, behold your mother!"

Let the simple beauty of it speak for itself: As Jesus assigns John the domestic responsibility of His mother's care, He was committing her to the hands of the disciple closest to Him, a responsibility that history records John was faithful to accept and fulfill. And in making the assignment, Jesus speaks to each of us in the bad days of our lives to refuse to allow our present pain to dull our sensitivity to the needs of others who depend on us. It demonstrates a magnificence I saw beautifully lived out by Vic after Cora died.

It had happened without warning on a Tuesday morning. Vic's bride of more than a half century, his partner through a lifetime of service to Christ as a pair of beloved and trusted leaders, was suddenly gone. A heart attack had taken her as she was ushered into eternal glory, and Vic was left, a bereaved husband.

He was never a whimperer on any terms. No one ever heard a word of complaint during those days following Cora's departure. In fact, Vic's failing physical condition, accompanied by the grief we all knew was cutting to the center of the soul of a man whose relationship with his wife was as near and dear as anyone could ever imagine, prompted most of us to suppose the obvious: "He'll follow her very, very soon."

Many of us have seen cases where lifelong closeness seems to have uniquely bonded a couple, and where physical weakness or sickness, joined to advanced years, puts life's conclusion within anticipatable nearness. When one is gone, the other often follows quickly.

We expected this with Vic; though not a welcome thought, it was nonetheless a reasonable one—their closeness, his grieving, his physical decline. *It will be soon*, most friends and family thought.

But Vic didn't follow at once.

I was a close friend to Vic and Cora and their children, as well as honored to be called Vic's pastor during the last decades of his life, so I went to spend time with him one day. The conversation was extended, without hurry and certainly without suggesting what many of us thought—that he would not survive long. But that day I encountered a man who was praying and willing to live "until I have a number of things settled." He was very businesslike and candid about it, acknowledging something on the order of the apostle Paul's words: "I am hard-pressed between the two, having a desire to depart and be with Christ, which is far better. Nevertheless to remain in the flesh is more needful for you" (Phil. 1:23–24).

There was nothing of arrogance or humanistic tenacity in his voice or in the stance of Vic's soul. His intent to pursue life was not a quest for emotional survival or a self-asserted will to live, as though he either desperately sought life or felt it his right to commandeer his destiny. Humanly speaking, he would have preferred "going home to heaven," but something else was much on his mind and fixed in his soul. I was deeply touched with a sense of paternal care, personal accountability, and spiritual passion in his whole demeanor.

During the following months, I stayed in touch with Vic. I seldom saw him, but heard from family: Vic was taking care of settling business matters, spending time with grandchildren, engaging in significant conversations with his children, phoning the few of his lifelong friends still alive—most in their eighth and ninth decades of life. And it was almost exactly nine months after Cora died that Vic's daughter called, suggesting I come to see him. "I think he's decided he's finished taking care of things, Jack," she said. And that's just about the same thing he said to me when we talked that last time.

Those nine months, like a pregnancy waiting to bring forth life, were completed, and Vic died. He had always been a man who cared and was concerned for people. Those characteristics made him a great spiritual leader. And at life's end, when the bad day of Cora's departure might have inclined him to surrender, he became a man with a yet-unfulfilled mission. In the pattern of his Savior, who still kept focus on the needs of those around Him while nailed to the ultimate bad day, Vic focused on life rather than his grief. He resolved issues concerning others near to him before he let go of life, before going to meet his Lord and to experience heaven's reunion with loved ones already gone ahead. In short, he did not let the bad days of his grieving interfere with his attendance to concerns regarding others who would be left behind.

Our Lord's discipling model speaks from this "word" spoken at Calvary: "Son . . . Mother." And it says: When you're going through a bad day, don't neglect taking care of those who are near to you. We all have a tendency to presume that those closest to us understand our dilemmas and that somehow they will automatically absorb them along with us. But that's not always the way it is.

How often does someone come home from a miserable day at work and transmit his irritation and anger to the kids or spouse? "If it has been a bad day for me, it's going to be bad for everybody." "If Mama [or Daddy] ain't happy, ain't nobody happy!" as the emblazoned sweatshirt says. But that can never be the spirit of a disciple of Jesus. Because I am His disciple, He will insist on my loss of any right to require those around me to pay the price of my frustration—no matter how close to me they are. His way is clear: If you're going through a bad day, be sure you take care of those near you. Don't transmit your trauma to them. They may share it with you (as Mary and John did with Jesus), but it shouldn't be dumped on them and they shouldn't be saddled with it involuntarily.

The best way to get through a bad day is the way that Jesus does it, and He is always more concerned with others than with Himself.

4

Aim Your Hard Questions
at God, Not Man

My God, My God, why have You forsaken Me?
—MATTHEW 27:46

Here is the fourth principle of how to live through a bad day: Aim your hard questions at God, not man. It is perhaps the most dramatic word spoken from Calvary. It trembles with emotional anguish, and nothing dramatizes it more passionately than the heart-piercing cry of God's Son, feeling a sense of abandonment at the darkest moment of this very bad day: "Why? Why? Why have You left Me now?"

The actual words Jesus cried out are quoted directly from Psalm 22, a song by then already a thousand years old—a lyric David prophesied before anyone could imagine God's Messiah would become the One to fulfill its agony. To glimpse a part of it, read with me:

My God, My God, why have You forsaken Me?
Why are You so far from helping Me,
And from the words of My groaning?
O My God, I cry in the daytime, but You do not
    hear;
And in the night season, and am not silent . . .
All those who see Me ridicule Me . . .
[They say,] "He trusted in the LORD, let Him
    rescue Him;
Let Him deliver Him, since He delights in
    Him!"
But You are He who took Me out of the womb . . .
I was cast upon You from birth . . .
Be not far from Me,
For trouble is near;

For there is none to help.
Many bulls have surrounded Me . . .
They gape at Me with their mouths,
Like a raging and roaring lion.
I am poured out like water,
And all My bones are out of joint;
My heart is like wax;
It has melted within Me.
My strength is dried up . . .
And My tongue clings to My jaws;
You have brought Me to the dust of death.
For dogs have surrounded Me;
The congregation of the wicked has enclosed Me.
They pierced My hands and My feet;
I can count all My bones.
They look and stare at Me . . .
But You, O LORD, do not be far from Me;
O My Strength, hasten to help Me! (vv. 1–2; 7–19)

That was the cry of the psalmist in the spirit of the
privileged candor that God welcomes from those who
worship Him. He welcomes tears in His presence, for

He isn't their source, and He allows complaints, for He alone can meet the needs. The counsel contained in Psalm 142 invites us to call in dark hours: "I cry out to the LORD with my voice . . . I pour out my complaint before Him" (vv. 1–2). Again, the message is clear: Aim your hard questions at God. You may not get the answer right then, but you can count on two things: (1) your cry never will fall on deaf ears, and (2) time will always bring an answer in your best interests. Always.

To scrutinize all the implications of this wrenching lamentation from Jesus' lips seems beyond human comprehension. We might be able to imagine the breaking in His voice or the anguish of His heart, but who can fathom the mystery of the separation taking place or the depth of the pain it struck to the soul of God's Son? This outcry born of inner agony was not a performance for melodramatic effect. No! The second person of the triune Godhead was experiencing a breach in the fellowship He had known with the eternal Father from before all worlds. And the separation— the cause of the forsakenness tearing at Jesus' mind—occurred because Jesus ("Him who knew no sin") was being made sin for us "that we might become the righteousness of God in Him" (2 Cor. 5:21).

This concept staggers the finest theological minds and boggles the imagination of any who thoughtfully weigh its reality. And though the Bible explains it in the words from 2 Corinthians, and though the psalmist prophesied it long before the Son became flesh to fulfill His saving mission on our behalf, I don't know that any human can grasp the deepest mystery of the moment, but I do know two things are clear.

First, as the Son of God, Jesus was suffering in Himself the divine fulfillment of the ancient lesson taught in the Old Testament image of the scapegoat— the sin-bearer creature that was cast out from the camp, carrying all the guilt of the people. In His death somehow Jesus was totally absorbing in Himself both the guilt and the penalty of all the sin of all the ages— a feat that can be explained only in that His qualifications as a *sinless* Savior provided space for *all sin* to be swallowed up in His person. Then in dying, He fully broke the power of sin to ever again rule anyone who puts his life within the redeeming circle of His resurrected life!

Second, as the Son of man, Jesus was wrestling with an inexplicably dark depression, transcending description and beyond survival except for the miraculous sustaining power of the Holy Spirit. That grace alone, Hebrews 9:14 tells us, enabled Him to complete the offering of Himself to God as sacrifice on our behalf. Yet notwithstanding His divinity and the divine strength accomplishing this eternal and cosmically encompassing feat, the Lamb of the Cross was fully human as well. And He was devastated by the vacuum void of the Father's presence—bitterly crying as He actually drank the cup He pleaded in Gethsemane to avoid.

This is the central moment of Calvary: It is the fourth of seven words. It is filled with questions, with darkness, with a sense of ultimate forsakenness—God forsaken! Even if we never experience the dimension of Jesus' depression, all of us have had moments when we have wondered, "Why, God?" And then we know we have a Savior who has been there and understands our despair, and we have His example pointing us in the right direction. When you're in the middle of a bad day—or worse, when you feel sure you've lost touch with heaven and are mystified in your loneliness—aim your hard questions at God, not man.

Why? Because in life's darkest hours, there are usually no human beings with adequate answers. Counselors may analyze; associates may sympathize; experienced friends may empathize. But finite minds and feeble flesh can never satisfy us with the Presence we seek, for we truly cry for God Himself, not answers. When "bad day blues" turn black with the unanswerable, and everything you thought you knew backfires, forget human philosophies or riddling theologies. Cry out to God. He doesn't mind our complaints, and although He may seem absent, He's never far away. Ask my friend Bill.

The deal had crashed. It involved a seven-digit, multimillion-dollar figure for his corporation. After months of careful planning on the human side, and after more than two years of prayerfully seeking God's will and wisdom on the divine side, Bill as CEO had led his company to the brink of a pivotal acquisition.

The funding was in place, and the promise of a broad range of new possibilities was open before them. The stockholders had been advised of the impending purchase, and the press was watching expectantly because of the innovation manifest in the development. And best of all, Bill's soul was clear before God as he moved forward with the plan.

Though the acquisition would advance profits dramatically, Bill knew his own heart before God. He had laid it before his Lord again and again during many months. He and his wife, Marie, had prayed together with unity and humility, "Dear Father, we want nothing but Your will—for our company, exactly as for our marriage. You are the Center of our lives: not success, not wealth, not recognition. We seek Your direction and blessing on Your terms, Lord. And whatever distills of profit or advancement, we present to You in its entirety, not as a bribe to secure Your blessing, but as a sacrifice to honor Your name."

Then somebody pulled the rug out from under everything. The whole world was disintegrating around him like a rocket exploding on a pad at Cape

Canaveral, the gantry tipping wildly from its base, its framework shattered and falling apart.

The whole deal threatened to collapse, and worse, the other company that had entered the agreement in apparent good faith had violated the carefully constructed terms and had secretly conspired to make Bill look like the culprit. Compounding his frustration was the fact that the other company's CEO claimed to be a Christian, and he was in many respects viewed as a man of spiritual values as well as moral principle. Driven by his fears and trapped in a newly surfaced but self-imposed difficulty, the other leader had turned the tables in a self-protective way that trashed the business agreement and proposed Bill as the cause of the problem. Bill was being named as the source of the deal's ruin. Bill's wisdom as a leader was in question, and his integrity as a businessman was being thrown toward the scrap pile. There was an "out," however.

The dishonesty of the other company—the calculated conspiracy that was besmirching Bill's good name—could easily be challenged in court. Bill only had to register his case and go public with charges that would vindicate him, even though the deal would be lost. At that point the Holy Spirit met Bill in his dilemma: God's Word summoned him beyond human wisdom to trust beyond tragedy.

The doubts of his shareholders were hanging over him like an impending cloudburst, and his employees were perplexed by negative reports on their otherwise trusted leader. Tempted to bitterness, stabbed with pain, torn by confusion, Bill cried out to God, "I don't get it! You know my heart. You know how I've sought You at every point. Why is this happening to me, Lord? I don't care about the loss of a potential expansion. You know that! But why have You thrown me out to the dogs of injustice?"

He laid before God's throne his complaint over the devastation of having sought God for direction, having received clarity and peace to proceed, and then seeming to have been forsaken by the One he had sought foremost to please. It was not a rebel's act of defiance but a child's cry of bewilderment. He bent over in prayer, doubled up with the physical torture of a soul driven to the edge. And one day during that season of his pained outcry before God's throne, God's Word resounded in his soul: "Do not take your brother to court. Do not defend yourself. Let Me be your Defender instead" (1 Cor. 6:1–7; Pss. 7:10; 59:16–17; 62:1–8).

Remembering the Savior's words in Psalm 22—the source of Jesus' cry from the Cross, "My God, My God!"—Bill was helped to wrestle through to his decision. His choice: "The deal may die, and my reputation be buried, but I will not defend myself." All human counsel would argue otherwise, but Bill determined to make God his sole point of complaint, inquiry, and defense. The outcome of his decision is almost too successful to be believed where human doubt, fear, and anger over injustice usually recommend reprisal and retribution. After an extended season, when things looked as if they would never change, during which Bill daily faced the need for keeping his commitment of trust to leave his case with God, a full resolution was realized. The deal was resurrected. No parties were embarrassed. All inequity was rectified. And Bill never publicly revealed the details of the whole story—not even afterward.

There is a price to making God your point of reference when the hard questions raised in the middle of a bad day rack your mind and torture your soul. It's the price of listening to His answers and deciding whether or not to submit to His way rather than your own. The rock-solid truth remains, the evidence of God's Word provides the unchanging, timeless assurance again and again: Your cry never will fall on deaf ears, and there will always be an answer—in His time—and that answer will be in your best interests. Always.

5

Be Human Enough to Acknowledge Your Need

I thirst!
—JOHN 19:28

Among the words Jesus spoke from the Cross, the fifth and sixth statements are uniquely linked. Although their content is radically different, the gospel record in John 19:28–30 makes it clear that Jesus asked for a drink for one primary reason. It wasn't the most obvious—simply slaking thirst—though the ordeal of crucifixion would be more than reason to cry out for a drink. The horrific energy drain, the perspiration amid trauma, the bloodletting—all would produce rapid dehydration. Jesus had earlier turned down the offer of a drink including a pain-dulling prescription that might have satiated a degree of thirst, but would likely have reduced mental acuity (Mark 15:23). Instead, the Lamb of Calvary chose to retain command of His senses; any escape from pain or other temporary comfort was not on His agenda.

The one reason Jesus asked for something to drink had to do with what He was about to say. The biblical setting made that unmistakably clear. As the Word incarnate was about to bring His final sermon—a message for all time, to first be proclaimed from the elevated pulpit of His Cross—He needed to clear His voice. The announcement to follow was not to be muttered or choked out but trumpeted so that all mankind throughout all history would be able to hear it. But to prepare for that moment, He needed help.

Let me emphasize this carefully, for there is a very practical point for our discipling lessons on this very, very bad day. Make no mistake, Jesus was dying, but

He was also fully in control of the moment. Everything taking place was *His* choice. It is true that He could summon an angel host to deliver Him. It is true that no one could take His life, but He chose to lay it down.

And that point—His capacity to choose as He willed—is central to our seeing the next truth as important for us when we go through hard days. Here it is: Jesus' plea for a drink is a reminder that no one is so in control, so spiritual, so self-sufficient, that he can make it through a bad day without people to help him.

The lesson for us all is centered in *why* Jesus made known His need, not only that He did. His purpose, as we have noted, was that there would be clarity in the statement He was about to make, and there are parallels to our bad days as well.

A bad day can blur your perspective and muddy your speech. It can fog the mind and bring uncertainty to your heart or tempt you to mutter words of dubious wisdom unless you are willing to let your need be known to others. On a bad day, humbling yourself to ask the assistance of others can help you clarify the stance you're taking in trusting God. This is no prompting to seek the shallow refuge of someone to pamper you by mouthing self-pitying complaints. But just as the drink offered to Jesus, though bitter, helped clarify the confession of faith He was about to bring, you and I need the help we can bring to each other.

That was certainly what Anna and I discovered following that dismal day the phone rang with the pathological report about the biopsy on the polyp removed from her colon.

Few things seem to paralyze faith more readily than one word: *cancer*. Retaining hope often seems a form of denial before the monstrous facts of this beast's ongoing harvest of multitudes. Notwithstanding the efforts of dedicated researchers and the advances made in battling this sinister opponent, when cancer touches your family, your world is suddenly clouded by a very bad day.

Neither of us will ever forget the long drive that afternoon after the phone call. The doctor was sensitive, kind, and understanding. But he was also professional, direct, and realistic. There were things that could be done: surgery to elect, postsurgical treatments to be determined, actions to take that offered no guarantees; only percentages of likely removal or remission could be quoted.

That bad day was a sunny, springtime afternoon, but the quiet beauty we had sought on our drive through the nearby mountains—to talk together with oft-quavering voices on the edge of tears before the worst of all prospects—was little comfort.

Though my left hand was always firm in its grip on the steering wheel, my right hand was in constant touch with Anna as we discussed all the possibilities. I held her hand lovingly and patted her knee assuringly. Sometimes I simply stroked her forearm, realizing the physical frame carrying the dearest person on earth to me also carried a death sentence within it.

Our conversation was not fatalistic. We have prayed for hundreds over the years, and we have seen many precious people healed—and also many die. We had excellent doctors caring for her, and we were certain their skills held the best possibilities. We also knew, above all, that her life—indeed, ours together— was in the hands of our loving Father. We have a loving family, too, and there was no question about their concern and support. But there was a question: How do we discuss this with the congregation?

There are certain difficulties wrapped in the high privilege of being entrusted with a very large church. Ten thousand members may sound impressive to the casual observer, but each one is simply another sheep in the pastures of the Great Shepherd. Despite the number who call you "Pastor," serving them as His sheep while serving Him as a sheep-become-shepherd requires wisdom in deciding how much of your burden you should share with them. For us, it was not a question of feeling obligated to demonstrate great optimism or expect God to vindicate our ministry with a miracle. Rather, it was the mixed feelings of concern that ran from (1) not wanting to exploit the emotions of the congregation in our interest when there are always so many others in the church who need love and support more than we do, from (2) hoping to avoid discouraging those feeble sheep who, being young or weak in faith, become stultified or unduly set back in their view of God if someone they deem beyond problems faces a huge one, to (3) wondering to what degree a public mention of Anna's disease would excite a rash of goodwilled but misguided approaches by those wanting to "come and lay healing hands on her" or those offering advice on alternative remedies. We were not ill-disposed toward any means by which anyone would propose care, but we were uncertain about how much traffic we could tolerate, however well intended, once word was given concerning her condition.

That day, we talked and prayed our way to the only conclusion we felt was consistent with both the Word and the Spirit of God, which have always been our ultimate points of reference. Over the next few days we met with key members of our staff, as well as the elders of our church, and spelled out the whole situation to them. We received their loving support, which was joined to their confirmation of our decision.

The Sunday following this process—eight days

after hearing the medical report—we presented ourselves to the whole congregation. The elders had pre-
pared for the Communion of the Lord's Table to be
served as we gathered in God's presence. I preceded
any mention of Anna's condition with a brief teaching
on the need of every member of Christ's body toward
the others (Rom. 12:4–5; 1 Cor. 12:12–26). Then I
related the facts pertaining to Anna's physical circumstance and spoke of our desire not to distract the congregation from larger issues by reason of their
affectionate concern over ours.

In short, like Jesus on the Cross, we were acknowledging our "thirst." It was not for personal attention
or for sincere, yet unsought pity, but for helping us to
clearly live out—to enunciate through wisdom prag-
matically applied in the face of a hard situation—a
declaration of faith, hope, and peace, whether by life
or by death.

It was one of the most memorable days in the life
of our congregation. There were tears, but they were
not born of either fear or discouragement. There were
Holy Spirit–prompted words of encouragement and

confidence amid trial, but they were not born of either religious excitement or legalistic triumphalism. There was joy at the Lord's Table where we partook together in remembrance of Calvary's victory beyond apparent loss and where we also embraced the promise of hope for healing. Elders anointed Anna with oil in the name of the Lord Jesus Christ, and the congregation rose with high praises to God for His Word, which undergirds us in all of life's trials and goes before us unto ultimate victory.

The results were manifest over the days, weeks, months, and years to follow. First, the congregation stood firm with us throughout the ordeal of Anna's surgery and postsurgical season, but they didn't capitulate to doting preoccupation or emotional distraction. Gracious concern was always present, but overweening attentiveness was thankfully absent.

And Anna was healed!

No, it wasn't instantly. Yes, the surgeon's hands were involved. No, we didn't experience immediate release from fears. Yes, great prayer and faith were exercised and brought enormous hope beyond reason and peace beyond explanation. And without question, there were marked events within the flow of the whole ordeal that exceeded human wisdom or skill, and there were results that our doctor was free to acknowledge as manifesting a gracious providence. In it all, that Providence, our loving Lord, transcended the best human care could accomplish and manifested His merciful hand in a complete recovery. Why? Not because of any worthiness on our part; certainly not without the partnership of an entire congregation who heard us say, "We need help to pursue our path with clarity and with faith."

Jesus' fifth word from Calvary calls us to learn this point of discipleship, especially when bad days come upon us. It is one thing to fortify ourselves and brace against the storms of life's bad days, but it is another to humbly acknowledge our need of each other. It's an inescapably important principle to apply: If the Son of God requested help during Calvary's struggle, I am wise to remember that I will have times I need to ask for help, for human assistance, as an avenue of divine grace. It is neither immature nor self-pitying. It is the balance taught in the words of Galatians 6, which seems to contradict itself, saying: "Each one shall bear his own load" (v. 5), after declaring, "Bear one another's burdens, and so fulfill the law of Christ" (v. 2). But the distinctive words of the original text contrast our personal "responsibilities" (v. 5) with the "overload" that life sometimes deals every one of us.

It's the very model seen in the person of Jesus. He wasn't seeking respite from responsibility; He needed help in the midst of physical overload. And when we look at the Savior crying, "I thirst!" we see yet another principle of how to live through a bad day. In tough times you need the help of others to enable and assist you to clarify your confession of your faith and trust in God's grace.

You'll also need to remember and acknowledge that. Humbly. Honestly.

6

Be Assured, There Is a Purpose and an End

It is finished!
—John 19:30

Tetelesthai—It is finished!

The most significant single word in the Greek New Testament translates to the most triumphant declaration. It contains both a prophecy and a verdict. Jesus, the Son, prophesied the momentarily impending conclusion of His saving work, and *even before the Cross's finale,* He anticipated the Father's verdict and His ultimate intervention.

The atoning sacrifice of the Lamb was accomplishing eternal salvation.

The deliverance of mankind was as possible as Israel's deliverance was from Egypt more than a millennium before.

The dawn of world redemption had broken, and with it the chains of human slavery to sin, shame, and condemnation were being shattered.

Though they were the most climactic, those were not the final words spoken by the Savior from the Cross. He would shortly commend His Spirit into the Father's hands. But He was already confident; His declaration of triumph was being registered. The grounds were now established at a dual dimension: welcoming fallen humans back into fellowship with the Father and driving back the powers of evil from their dark and damning rule over mankind.

The essence of the magnificence in these words is their finality as a statement of faith. The ultimatum they declared was absolute, even though the victory was not yet visible. "It is finished!" was the Son of God's invitation to join Him in the conviction that now—

because of the Cross—there is nothing we struggle with that is without either a purpose or an end.

No struggle need ever again be pointless.

No suffering need ever again be unending.

The Master not only announced salvation's total accomplishment, but near the climax of His bad day, He summoned us to embrace this truth when we're agonizing through ours. He was teaching us to learn and live in this light:

First, we never face any assault of flesh, devil, circumstance, or personal weakness, but that God's hand is present, mighty, and available to work through it all and beyond it all. This doesn't mean God has planned every bad thing that happens to people. Evil things that are initiated by hell's hatefulness or by human sin, failure, and rebellion create their own problems. But beyond them all, God's ultimate deliverance is our promised inheritance.

Second, Jesus' words "It is finished!" are to lead us to understand that even before our personal ordeals are over, we are privileged to invite God's sovereign presence and power to invade our bad days, releasing

His triumphant grace to achieve His purposes in the end. The most incredible proposition in the universe is that the Sovereign of all creation awaits the invitation of frail humans. But once invited, the Father's transcendent power is ready to intervene—introducing a wisdom and might greater than anything producing the worst of our bad days.

The Cross demonstrates this point. When you're living through a bad day, don't expect to be able to "read" the full dimensions of God's redemptive plan in the middle of your struggle, but never doubt the certainty that it is in process. His call, "It is finished!" is our call to hold firm in this assurance: His sovereign power will ultimately win the day.

Karl and Pamela's baby died. The ordeal had been in progress for months. A horrible tumorous intrusion was crowding into the tiny infant's cranium, and at daybreak that Sunday morning the phone rang at our house. I spoke brief words of sympathy to the family friend who had called, advising me that the baby had succumbed to death, and almost immediately I left for the hospital. Karl and Pam were a strong pair in our congregation; they were parents already to three children, and they had so anticipated baby Jason's recovery, which would maintain a "two boys and two girls" evenness in the family.

I had wept with them the day before, bowing in prayer and uttering the one phrase the Lord had put on my lips: "Sustain this little boy *unto life*, O Lord, *unto life!*" I could not pray anything else, and I didn't give any interpretation to what I did pray. I have heard wonderful reports of miracles, especially in cases involving children, where God's creative reconstructive interventions have turned apparently futile circumstances into triumphant ones. We have had a small share in experiencing some of those miracles in our church family, but I have never felt it my privilege or assignment to declare one in advance of its occurring. Still, I had passionately prayed, "Unto life! Unto life!" But on the morning after, I was on my way to comfort a couple in a situation where death seemed to have won.

I turned the corner out of the subdivision where we lived, and I was slowing down to stop at the intersection's flashing red signal. It was still early, there was no other traffic, and as I slowed, I noticed a small object in the roadway. As I drew up to the crosswalk (there were no cars behind to goad me on after my stop), I got out to see what it was because I felt strangely moved to do so. There is no way to explain either my prompting or the scene that I saw other than to attribute it to the living God, who works signs as well as wonders. A dead sparrow lay there in the street—its head completely removed! The instant I saw it, a Voice deep within me—unprompted by human reason—whispered a message with clarity and conciseness: *Not one of them falls to the ground apart from your Father's will . . . Do not fear therefore; you are of more value than many sparrows* (Matt. 10:29, 31).

Returning to the driver's seat, I resumed driving to the hospital, my eyes brimming with tears and my mind racing even while my spirit soared with a deep sense of heaven's purpose invading Karl and Pam's moment. Whatever anyone else might say, I knew I had seen a sign, for there was no explanation why the bird would be lying there headless unless some purpose of God had arranged it. If a cat had snatched the bird and taken its head, it would have consumed the whole body. If a car had run over the bird, the head would have been on the pavement. Whatever happened—and at a timing that coincided with my arrival at the intersection—a message was clearly spoken to me: *This baby whose head was taken is gone, but Father God wants you to be reminded that the child is precious to Him and that he is of great value to the Father!*

That I felt this so profoundly was one thing, but how to relate it to a bereaved couple was another. It seemed to me that notwithstanding anything within my conviction, it could strike them as painfully contrived. But my uncertainty was instantly removed when I walked into the hospital room where Karl, Pam, and the couple who called me were embracing one another—praising God and worshiping Him for His goodness! They were not religious fanatics who blithely philosophized tragedy with a happy smile and a trite quoting of something like, "Everything is okay if you believe it's true." They were people who had been caught in the grip of God's grace and who had been persuaded by the Holy Spirit's comforting presence that beyond the tragedy, God was at work doing something grand. They didn't blame God or a deficiency of faith in Him for the event. They weren't bantering theological catchphrases or philosophical opinions. They had been secured in the arms of the Father and assured by the steadying pulse beat of His heart: *There is a purpose to unfold from Jason's short life, and there will be an end to your sorrow as well.*

Greeted with their warm embraces, I listened to their description of God's gentle preparation of their hearts for the baby's passing, and I prayed with praise alongside them. Then sensing the presence of the Holy Spirit's having worked such a wonder in the two bereaved hearts, I ventured telling of my experience while driving to the hospital. The response was, by now, predictable. No one needed to strain to make room for the episode, as though his spirituality was being tested by the response. They were stirred: "Indeed, Pastor Jack, the Lord is emphasizing the point. He has not only worked redemptively here in removing the pain of death's sting from our hearts in this moment; He is confirming to us that there is a purpose in this, not just a tragedy."

"From Tragedy to Triumph" suddenly became the theme of the day. The moment was so visited by divine grace, I couldn't help risking a suggestion: "Karl . . . Pam, let me ask your permission on something. I don't want to do anything that would risk appearing to exploit the emotion of the moment, but may I ask: Would you feel offended if I shared the story of this ordeal, along with this morning's events, with the congregation?" I could hardly believe my own ears. It was 6:45, and the first service would begin in forty-five minutes. I had a message ready, but I felt God had another one for our church family that day. Karl and Pam agreed, and the rest, to adapt a phrase, "is all He wrote!"

God inscribed a holy memory into the life of an entire congregation that day. He answered the doubts of people who wonder about premature death. He neutralized the superstitions that cause people to feel obligated to say God "designs" this kind of human agony. He fit together a combination of biblical good sense with human understanding. The result was not only a swelling of praise to God for His triumphs amid apparent tragedies, but that morning, more than thirty-five people received Jesus Christ as their Savior! (Yes, I did tell the sparrow story, and yes, the Holy Spirit made it credible to all hearts present, not as a rationalization but as a gracious illuminating providence reminding us of God's very personal care for each of us.)

His personal care is the reason that the events of any of life's bad days are a potential staging ground for the wonder of His redemptive working and a time you may witness signs of His personal attentiveness and care. When you're living through a bad day, there's a reason to declare, "It is finished!" All His purposes are secured and will be fulfilled, and whatever the present suffering, there is an end.

> Weeping may endure for a night,
> But joy comes in the morning. (Ps. 30:5)

7

Finally Surrender Your Day
to God, and Let It Go

Into Your hands I commit My spirit.

—Luke 23:46

When you come to the end of any day that's been a hard day, it's usually as difficult to conclude as it has been to live. The end of the day can be the start of a long night of reliving the day's struggle and of missing the restorative powers of sleep through the restlessness of a night as bad as the day. This principle of discipleship after the manner of our Savior becomes all the more important when you know the day you're ending might not be much different from tomorrow. Bad days can be weeks long, and the constituted agenda may not be rapid in its passing. Some things never go away fast enough, and the soul—the heart, mind, and emotions—can become preoccupied to the point that they wheel over and over with the same cycle of thoughts, the same pinching of pain, the same specter of fear, or the same bewildering doubts. And all of it attended by the relentless question, "When will all of this go away?"

To live through a bad day—indeed, to conclude it—is to place it into the hands of God and leave it there. That was how the agony of Calvary came to its conclusion, and it is important to understand what these words *didn't* mean as well as what they did. On the lips of Jesus, "Into Your hands I commit My spirit" is no more an act of wearied resignation than "It is finished!" was a cry of defeat. Both are assertions, statements of definitive action. The sixth word was one of *triumph*, the seventh one of *trust*.

Looking to the Cross, let it never pass our notice that the dying Lamb is also the Prince of life. The sacrifice is also the priest—Jesus Himself being, at once, the presented atonement and the presenting officiant. His was the life being laid down; He was the One laying down His life. And the hours of agony accomplished their purpose: The Atoning blood was shed, and the grace of forgiveness was initiated on eternally worthy grounds, for salvation was all but paid for. The blood of the Lamb was shed, and all that remained was His final surrender of life itself. Months earlier, Jesus had made a categorical statement on the subject: "I lay down My life that I may take it again. No one takes it from Me, but I lay it down of Myself" (John 10:17–18). Now that moment had come.

There is something preciously sublime about Jesus' final words from the Cross. Not only are they generally overlooked, but to overlook them is to miss their message for us as His disciples. From the human perspective His words indicate a colossal act of trust in the Father. He was surrendering His control of life into the Father's hands, whereas an hour before, He was torn with the agony of abandonment, feeling the distance between Himself as the bearer of our sin and the pure holiness of the Father, who is incapable of countenancing sin. But with nothing more than His confidence in the Father's fidelity to His own Word, the Son said, "I'm ready to release My hold on life, and I'm unafraid to do so because I am placing everything about Myself into Your hands." His words of trust, surrendering everything into the strong hands of the almighty God, are His concluding lesson to us about how to live through a bad day.

Trina sat in my office, the picture of composure. An attractive woman in her early forties and the wife of a successful physician, she was the essence of social grace and cultural sophistication. But there was nothing in her of the snobbishness or superiority that undermines the true dignity of a person with such regal bearing because Trina was a deeply devoted servant of the Savior. She had come to Christ several years ago, and her growth had been marked by a humility as surely as her background had cultivated in her that gentle dignity. But Trina's husband had never come to the Lord.

I had seen Walt in church a few times, and I had

met him once. Two things were clear. First, he had genuine respect and an almost reverent regard for his wife's faith. It wasn't the formal respect that polite society requires, but a manifest esteem for a dimension of life he recognized she possessed, which contributed something valuable to their home and marriage. But there was a second thing—the evidence of a subtle deception that suggests to an otherwise reasonable mind that somehow, "You don't need 'this' [that is, this Savior, Jesus]," or more honestly put, "If you ever open to Him, it will mean *genuine transformation*, and you don't want to stop being who you really are, do you?" It was in Walt's face—a fundamental dishonesty with himself—the inevitable result of a knowing soul being dishonest with God and knowing that too.

But this was another day, a day at least three years into Trina's walk with Christ, and she had asked to see me. She was direct and to the point: "Pastor Jack, I want to ask more for your prayer than for your counsel, and it relates to something I feel convinced I am to do. I know it will seem radical, and by any definition, I suppose it is. I don't want to seem to have taken leave of my senses, but I don't know anyone I can tell—nor do I plan to tell anyone else, other than Lisa, my closest friend.

"You've met Walt, and you know what a fine man he is. You also know that he isn't a Christian, notwithstanding his open acknowledgment to me that he knows he should give his heart to the Lord. I think you know me well enough to know I am not the nagging, religious wife type, and by God's grace, I believe I have obeyed the Word of God in the way I have *lived* and *loved* as a wife should. Walt does acknowledge this, and he has regularly expressed his gratefulness for my continued care for and attentiveness to him."

I was ready for the point to be made—one all too frequently asserted today by Christian spouses who say, "I've done everything I can, and I'm tired of trying: I want to get a divorce from my unbelieving wife (husband)." But I was spun for a complete loop when Trina continued the explanation of her prayer request.

"Pastor," she said and lowered her eyes with slight embarrassment, "I don't want to seem at all inappropriate to you, nor do I wish to make this any more awkward than it already is for me. The fact is, Walt is having an affair. I recently discovered this as the result of finding some medication he left on the cabinet—medicine for the treatment of venereal disease.

"When I confronted him about it, he admitted having the affair and having contracted the disease from the woman."

"Presuming you and he have been pursuing your normal sexual relationship," I inquired, "what in the world did he say to you in the light of your finding this out—seeing that he is now exposing you to the same disease?"

She responded, "He was a mix of shame and humiliation. He raised no argument for himself, apologized for the craziness of his behavior, and yet went on to say that as ashamed as he is, he couldn't promise he wouldn't yield again to the same temptation."

"Then I suppose your prayer request is that I begin urgent prayer that Walt take this signal of his foolishness to drive him to the Lord," I suggested.

She affirmed the desirability of such continued

prayer but went on to say that the real request was for her physical protection. "You see, Pastor Jack, I believe I have every right to walk away from Walt or to at least deny him bedroom rights until, first, he is cleared of the infection and, second, he has called it quits with the woman."

I nodded my agreement, but she wasn't finished. "I also believe the Lord is calling me to demonstrate my love for Walt in a way that will make an inescapable statement about God's love for him. Pastor, I believe I am to remain sexually available to him, even though it could be at the risk of my life." She further described having found a magazine with photos of naked males in pornographic interplay and wondered if Walt might be dabbling in ways that could even lead to her being exposed to AIDS.

"I know it's radical, Pastor. And I hope you will understand that my compulsion is something I believe the Lord has prompted me with, not some desperate need on my part to sustain sexual activity or to clutch for my husband's affection. I can survive without the physical relationship, and I don't have any doubt that Walt cares about me. The problem is, he is a horribly blinded soul, and my hope is that 'loving him as Jesus loves us,' that is 'while we were yet sinners, Christ died for us,' might shock him into reality with the awfulness of his being lost. He's a bound soul. But he's my husband, and I want to do anything I can to help him come to Christ."

I was as moved as I have ever been by one person's sense of marital commitment. Nothing—let me repeat—*nothing* in the Bible required this kind of caring on Trina's part; indeed, she had a biblical license to walk away from Walt. And *nothing* in my experience with dedicated followers of Jesus had ever surfaced a greater will or more dramatic commitment to self-sacrificing love for someone needing Christ. The words that came to mind as I prayed for her safety as she moved forward in this commitment were, "Father, into Your hands we commit Trina's life." They were the only hands that could shield her and secure her tomorrows.

A year or so later, Walt left Trina. He chose a promiscuous and perverted life instead of Christ—and the devotedly marvelous woman he had as his wife. And Trina? She was never infected, though she continued as her husband's lover and faithful wife until the day he announced he was leaving. She kept her life constant in Christ, and though I haven't seen her for years, she still has a strong relationship with her children and with her Savior.

I have never proposed Trina's "surrender" as a model to anyone, but it certainly strikes an opposite chord to the readiness with which many Christian believers will walk away from their marriages today, saying things have "gone bad." And marriage isn't the only arena in which we are often called to live through bad days. There are dozens of life issues that call us to follow Jesus' pathway in living through a bad day; issues that are seldom as quick to pass as we could wish and that always call us to the Cross to hear the Savior's words again and again.

In Philippians 3 the apostle Paul expressed a life-long goal to know Christ in "the power of His resurrection," a goal to experience the dynamism of the supernatural dimension of life that Jesus called "abundant"—the life He came to bring to us all. But those words do not stand alone. They have a companion phrase that points the pathway to "knowing Christ" in abundant life power, for the sentence ends, ". . . and the fellowship of His sufferings, being conformed to His death" (v. 10). The charted course is clear. It is and always has been called "the way of the Cross."

The Cross not only calls us to *Jesus,* who alone is the Way, the Truth, and the Life—who alone holds the keys of eternal life and calls us to receive His forgiveness and power through our repentance for sin and faith in Him as God's Son, the only Savior. The Cross also calls us to *a life,* to the wisdom of God's ways in all our relationships and pursuits, and to the pattern of Jesus' model in the face of our deepest struggles and most difficult trials. The same One who died to offer us abundant life in our todays—and eternal life in tomorrow's forever—addressed history's consummate bad day in a way that teaches us how we might face ours.

- Forgive anyone—no, *everyone*—who seems set on ruining your life.

- Though beset yourself, focus on encouraging others who are struggling and uncertain.

- Be sure you are sensitive and loving, certain to take care of those who are near you.

- When seemingly impossible questions come, aim them at God, not at man.

- Whatever your adequacy, never be above making known your need for help.

- Embrace the certainty that God's "finishes" *always* have a purpose and an end.

And finally when it is all said, one thing remains to be done:

- Surrender everything to God and let go.

It's how to live through a bad day.

OTHER BOOKS BY JACK HAYFORD

The Beauty of Spiritual Language:
Unveiling the Mystery of Speaking in Tongues

There are few other topics on which Christians are so divided. And a large majority of believers are unclear about what spiritual language really means. This is a balanced, biblical approach for anyone wanting to make an honest inquiry into the nature of speaking in tongues. Hayford debunks common myths surrounding the practice of tongues and shares with readers the beauty and the order of spiritual language that he has discovered during his times of private communion with God. • ISBN: 0-7852-7268-2

E-Quake:
A New Approach to Understanding the End Times Mysteries in the Book of Revelation

Pastor Jack Hayford believes the key to understanding the book of Revelation is to understand and correctly interpret the time and events surrounding the major earthquakes in Revelation. In *E-Quake* Pastor Hayford offers a practical study of the book of Revelation, not a speculative or sensationalized look at prophecy. Readers will understand how this revelation of Jesus Christ affects their lives today.
• ISBN: 0-7852-7472-3